PR Tools to Toot Your Own Horn

PR Tools to Toot Your Own Horn

Strategies and Ideas for Low-Cost Small Business Public Relations

By Diane Seltzer

Printed in the United States of America

ISBN-13: 978-1481143554

ISBN-10: 1481143557

This book is dedicated to courageous small business owners and entrepreneurs who are living their dream of growing a business into something great.
You inspire me every day.

-    D.S.

Table of Contents

Introduction

Whether you are an entrepreneur, owner-operated small business, "solopreneur" or simply have limited staff and resources, you most likely need to create and manage your own public relations strategies and initiatives.

If you don't toot your own horn, who will?

But like many small businesses, you probably need some help understanding how to fully maximize your public relations potential... to maximize both your efforts and your budget.

Luckily for small businesses like yours, developing and executing on public relations strategies to advance business goals doesn't necessarily require the help or expense of a PR agency. In fact, there are many PR tools and strategies that small businesses can tap into to help them accomplish measurable results in public relations on their own... without breaking the bank.

Most small business owners are also uniquely positioned to manage their own PR because they ARE the experts in their business and industry. Nobody understands what they do and what they bring to their industry or local market than the small business owner. This deep business knowledge and industry expertise often makes an individual business owner the best spokesperson or advocate for promoting their own business.

With the right PR marketing tools, strategies and tactics, any small business can do it.

It's time to toot your own horn.

Why I wrote *PR Tools to Toot Your Own Horn*

I've spent nearly 20 years finding and using low-cost marketing tools for my employers as a corporate marketing manager, and then for my clients as a marketing consultant. Naturally, PR has always been an important part of the marketing mix because public relations initiatives typically gave us the biggest return on our investment (whether it was time or money that was invested).

As a corporate marketing manager I was lucky enough to work with top PR agencies that acted as an extension of our in-house marketing team. Working with some of the best PR experts in the industry I learned a lot of the tricks of the trade... like how to develop and execute on PR strategies and how to make the most of PR opportunities with both old and new media.

Having the assistance of a PR agency during my corporate marketing days was arguably a luxury that many smaller businesses with smaller marketing budgets just do not have. As a marketing consultant I now use many of the strategies and tactics I learned from managing an outside PR team to stretch a small business marketing budget.

One thing I have found throughout my career is that EVERY company – no matter what size – can benefit from a good marketing tool that gives businesses tangible results. But of course this is especially important for small businesses that have tight budgets for marketing and growing their business.

They can't afford expensive consultants, large marketing staffs or infrastructure investments. Without easy to use, low-cost tools small businesses can often fall behind the curve and struggle with competition.

This thought process – identifying low-cost tools and resources for small businesses to leverage – was the original inspiration for my website *Small Business Marketing Tools* (www.SBMarketingTools.com), as well as the inspiration for this book.

Because PR is an important part of helping a business get off the ground and grow, I wanted to put together a book dedicated to ways small businesses can leverage PR tools – strategies, ideas, tactics and reliable services to help them implement PR initiatives. This book is intended to be an easy reference for small businesses looking to build on a PR strategy and be inspired by new ideas to generate buzz and grow their business.

Focus of *PR Tools to Toot Your Own Horn* book

Throughout this book, I will review basic public relations strategies along with some of the best free or low-cost PR tools and resources that I have found useful for small businesses. Each section includes thorough examples of how to execute simple, yet effective, PR strategies.

Most importantly, the ideas discussed in this book are straight-forward, easy-to-follow strategies that any small business can use on their own.

Links to recommended tools, website resources and other books for in-depth reading on specific topics can be found in a full directory at the end of this book.

The book also includes a link to a FREE downloadable package of bonus PR tools I have developed to guide you through some key areas of public relations. These bonus tools include a Press Release Checklist, Press Release Template and a Media Outreach Guide.

Finally, to help cut through some of the industry jargon (some words used in this book, as well as other terms you may hear elsewhere), I have included a glossary of common PR terms to use as a reference with this book and your PR plans.

PR Tools to Toot Your Own Horn is the first in a series of books by *Small Business Marketing Tools* – a website focused exclusively on highlighting low-cost tools, strategies and resources for small business marketing and productivity.

You can keep updated on the latest small business marketing tools and resources – as well as new book titles – on my Small Business Marketing Tools website www.SBMarketingTools.com.

Chapter 1: Define Public Relations for Your Business

Before we start discussing public relations tools and strategies, it's important to get grounded on what exactly public relations means to you and your small business.

Public relations can affect a business in many ways. It can help generate awareness, build brand recognition, influence consumer perception and lead to more sales and revenue opportunities for a company. Good public relations can mean the difference between fighting an uphill battle with your business and gliding your way to the top of your industry niche.

Unfortunately, many small businesses don't understand how to begin to leverage public relations by building PR objectives, strategies and tactics. Properly defining what public relations means to your business is the first step in developing strategies and tactics that will produce positive PR results.

The art of public relations takes time and patience – successful results don't typically come overnight from just one carefully executed tactic. Rather, success in public relations comes from charting a course with multiple tactics and tools that work together to reach overall business goals.

With a basic understanding of the definition of public relations, businesses can begin to create PR marketing plans and strategies aimed at influencing public perception, creating media exposure and ultimately advancing their business goals.

So let's start by getting back to the basics.

Basic Definitions of Public Relations

Public relations can mean many things to businesses. Simple definitions that often come to mind when asked how to define PR include:

- Proactively influencing public perception of a company

- Generating public exposure or publicity for a company

- Garnering media or press coverage of company news, products or events

- Effectively handling negative company news or incidents publicly

Other authoritative resources offer some basic "textbook" definitions of public relations that are worth reviewing:

- According to a classic textbook on marketing, *Marketing* by Peter D. Bennett, "public relations" is an intentional effort to produce favorable un-paid communication (as opposed to paid publicity or advertising) with an organization's stakeholders (such as employees, customers, clients, stockholders or the public at large).

- The Public Relations Society of America (PRSA), the world's largest and foremost organization of public relations professionals, has created an even simpler definition of public relations that is widely accepted among PR professionals. Their official definition states: "Public relations helps an organization and its publics adapt mutually to each other."

PRSA also recognizes that modern day public relations activity has evolved with changing roles and technological advances (such as social media and the internet) to emphasize concepts of "engagement" and "relationship building".

Public relations also involves effectively managing the overall image of an organization with proactive outreach and quick action to mitigate any actions that may harm the public's perception of an organization. By positively influencing public perception, public relations can be a very effective marketing tool.

The result of generating industry exposure and positive customer perceptions often leads to many tangible business benefits, including:

- Increased website visits

- Increased lead inquiries

- Increased sales opportunities

- Improved customer loyalty

- New partnerships, distribution channels or investors

What Public Relations Does NOT Mean

Public relations is not advertising. Although there are certainly promotional aspects to public relations, in the end you really can't buy good PR.

As a business you can make investments in activities or strategies that will generate good PR, tactics that can persuade public or media opinion or programs that will result in positive customer reactions. Good PR needs to be earned by communicating and influencing public perception of your company.

There are some publications that have a fuzzy line between editorial coverage and advertising. With today's digital age, many print publications are hurting for advertising dollars and may try to get you to pay for editorial coverage – or offer "free editorial coverage" with advertising buys. In these cases, the PR is more of an advertorial (hybrid of advertising and editorial). While it is perfectly acceptable to pay for editorial if you really want the coverage, publications should not pressure a company to advertise in exchange for editorial coverage.

The Importance of Low-Cost PR Tools for Small Businesses

With tight marketing budgets and staff resources, leveraging easy-to-use and low-cost marketing tools is essential for businesses to compete and survive.

There are many ways small businesses can get the impact of a big marketing budget without the time or cost investment. In fact, even many large businesses are even tapping into free or low-cost marketing tools because of their ease of use, quick implementation and ability to achieve measurable results on a small or limited budget.

Knowing how to find and use the right PR tools that are cost-effective for your business is the key to being successful on a budget.

A basic understanding of PR principles – combined with some strategies, ideas and tips on how to leverage low-cost PR tools – can help ANY business learn how to get big business results in public relations on a small business budget.

Public Relations Focus in this book

In this book, the focus will be on PR tools that can influence public opinion of small businesses and strategies you can use in the process. These PR tools, strategies and ideas are aimed at generating industry exposure and positive reactions by customers and media/press representatives – a major priority for small businesses looking to build their brand and reputation within a local market or industry niche.

We'll spend a bit of time on press releases because that is such a big part of generating media coverage and buzz for your business. And there's much more involved in press releases than just generating the release… you need to decide what news is worthy of a release, how best to distribute it and how to get the attention of journalists. Our free bonus PR checklist tool will help walk you through the creation, distribution and promotion of your press releases.

Media outreach takes a big commitment to get good coverage for your business. We'll review how to build relationships with key media contacts and journalists as well as developing specific strategies for each target media outlet. A media outreach guide is available at as another free bonus PR tool to download and keep you on track with media outreach contacts and strategies.

Of course you'll also learn a lot about how to use social media with public relations activities. Social media has become one of the biggest low-cost PR tools for small businesses to tap into and really make a difference for their businesses. Learn specific strategies and tactics for each of the major social media sites (like Facebook, Twitter and LinkedIn) so that you can keep your company in the spotlight.

If you are a locally focused business we'll touch on how to define PR goals and strategies for local use... and take advantage of special local event opportunities.

Finally, we'll focus on next steps to keep generating new opportunities for your PR pipeline... and generating more buzz for your business. We'll leave you thinking about how you can build PR opportunities into annual marketing plans and create an ongoing pipeline to keep the momentum going.

Chapter 2: How to Build a PR Strategy

Running around tooting your own horn without a plan would be like conducting an orchestra without having any sheet music. It would be like trying to sing a song without first writing the lyrics.

Well, you get the idea. You'd just be creating a whole lot of noise and hoping the right people hear you. Without a clear PR plan and strategy you could just be wasting your breath tooting your own horn (and wasting time and money!)

You wouldn't try to run your business without a business plan... and you shouldn't try to run your public relations without a marketing and PR plan. I am a big fan of putting a plan on paper. It keeps you on track, focused and accountable.

Define PR Goals and Objectives for Your Business

Before rolling out specific strategies and tactics, businesses should strive to develop specific goals and objectives for their public relations. Public relations goals and objectives are often intertwined with many other strategies and tactics within a marketing plan... which should be based on the overall goals and objectives for a business.

So what exactly is the difference between "goals" and "objectives"? These are terms that many people tend to use interchangeably, but they are really quite different.

A marketing **OBJECTIVE** is a mission or purpose and is actually broader in scope than goals. Objectives are typically qualitative and are supported by more measurable quantitative goals, and may even be comprised of several different goals.

Examples of PR objectives for a business may include:

- Improving public perception and recognition of a company

- Securing print or online media coverage of company news, products or events

- Reducing or eliminating negative company press

A marketing **GOAL** is defined as a desired result or specific achievement. Typically a goal is a measurable result that is achieved through marketing objectives. Because goals are quantitative, a business can always clearly answer whether or not a marketing goal was met with a simple yes or no.

Examples of PR goals for a business may include:

- Release 1 press release per quarter

- Secure editorial coverage in top 3 publications

Of course in some cases public relations efforts can be difficult to measure and tie back to specific goals and objectives. Public perception, for example, is a difficult factor to measure and can be somewhat subjective. But as a small business in tune with your customers and industry, positive movement in public perception can often be measured in terms of increased business, customer testimonials and general public interest.

Assessing PR Goals and Objectives

Your PR goals and strategies may not always be the same year over year and throughout your business life cycle.

For start-ups, PR goals and objectives will likely be aligned with creating awareness in a target market. As the business grows, your main PR goals may transition to more targeted awareness or a more specific perception in the market (like being known as a thought-leader or industry expert).

Each year you will need to evaluate your PR strategies and re-align them with business goals and objectives to ensure you are focusing your efforts on the most important strategies. This is important for any business, but especially important when you have limited funds and resources.

PR Strategy - Where to Focus Public Relations Efforts

Most small businesses with limited budgets will focus their public relations efforts on generating industry exposure and positive reactions by customers and media/press representatives.

A major priority for many small businesses is to build their brand and reputation within a local market or industry niche with the assistance of public relations strategies and tactics. A strong brand often leads to improved business opportunities, partnerships or equity investments for a growing small business.

The strategies and tactics used to implement public relations goals and objectives can include things like:

- Targeting industry trade media coverage

- Implementing social media outreach efforts

- Staging PR events and media opportunities

In addition to standard press releases and media outreach, the adoption of social media in public relations has now become a mainstream strategy for PR professionals to meet their business objectives. And the cost-effectiveness of social media is a big bonus for small businesses. This will be covered more in the Social Media for PR section.

Creating an Integrated PR Strategy

One of the biggest reasons public relations is so important for small businesses is the fact that it has minimal impact on a tight marketing budget. In fact, PR is often referred to as "free press".

Of course this so-called free press is valuable to businesses of any size, but it is especially valuable to small businesses on a shoestring budget that are trying to compete against bigger companies with bigger budgets.

The idea of "free press" also helps to stretch a marketing budget by supporting other paid opportunities and making them even more effective. You can get more bang for your buck by using an integrated marketing approach that leverages some paid marketing activities with free activities like public relations.

For example, customers will be more receptive to print advertisements or direct mail when the piece is preceded by some good PR buzz, industry media coverage or editorial within the publication.

Making a concerted effort to capture a free editorial opportunity alongside a paid print advertisement can reap benefits two-fold.

If you are purchasing an ad in a publication, inquire about editorial opportunities. Although it's not supposed to happen, many editorial teams will favor paid advertisers. And the opposite is also true - if you secure an editorial spot in a publication, an accompanying ad might be a good idea to leverage the "free press" coverage.

Overall, the messages you communicate in your PR efforts should be replicated across all your marketing activities... supporting each other in an integrated fashion.

Chapter 3: Managing PR In-House vs. Hiring an Agency

OK, so you understand the basics of PR, you put together a strategy... so now it's easy to manage it all, right?

You may be wondering... can I really toot my own horn? Or do I need help from a professional?

Let's face it – most small businesses cannot afford to hire an agency to manage their public relations activities. And in today's world of social media and self-serve marketing tools, I am not entirely convinced a public relations agency is even necessary for most businesses (of any size, let alone small).

In most cases, businesses that take the time to develop a basic understanding of public relations strategies CAN handle the typical roles or duties of an agency on their own.

Let's break it down so you understand what these roles are and how you might be able to manage these activities for your own business.

Typical Roles of an Outside PR Agency

When deciding whether or not to hire an outside PR agency it is helpful to understand some of the roles agencies typically play in helping a business and whether or not adequate PR tools are available to use independent of an agency.

Here are some typical agency roles and potential PR tools and strategies you can leverage on your own to accomplish the tasks typically handled by an agency:

PR Agency role: Press release writing

PR Tool / Strategy: If you have never written a press release before it may seem daunting, but there are many guides to writing a press release – including one covered in this book – that make writing them fairly straightforward. There is no reason why a business can't write a press release by following a standard template approach.

The only caveat is having someone on your staff that has the ability to write well enough to represent your company and your announcement in a professional way. Typically a marketing team member or freelance writer has the skill set to accomplish this task, or as a business owner you may have business writing skills yourself.

PR Agency role: Press release distribution

PR Tool / Strategy: Outside of the agency world, this PR task may seem overwhelming. But the fact is that distributing a press release is one of the simpler tasks of public relations – especially in recent years with the availability of press release distribution services that any experience level can utilize.

Most of these services are very low-cost and easy to use
– designed to be self-serve public relations tools for
small businesses. Press release distribution services
and tools (like PR Web, eReleases or 24/7 Press
Releases) can reach general media contacts, industry
news outlets, search engines and social media outlets.
Options and specific press release distribution tools are
covered in the Press Release Distribution section of this
book.

PR Agency role: Media outreach

PR Tool / Strategy: Media outreach for editorial
coverage in publications (also known as "pitching"
journalists) can be time consuming and requires
persistence… but it is a skill that anyone can develop.

If your market niche is small – like a select industry
segment or a local geographic area – developing
relationships with your key media contacts for potential
coverage is manageable. It's all about developing
relationships with journalists, helping them understand
your expertise, and how you (or your business) adds
value to their editorial coverage. See more guidance in
the Media Outreach section of this book.

PR Agency role: Writing editorial/Matte releases

PR Tool / Strategy: Many publications will accept fully
written articles or stories that PR professionals submit
(known as "matte releases") to fill publication space
when content is needed. Although PR agencies have
seasoned editorial writers, sometimes no one can tell
your story quite as well as you. The trick is finding the
"newsworthy" angle and then writing editorial

submissions (stories or articles) in an engaging way to entice an editor to pick it up for a publication.

Although there are no off-the-shelf PR tools that can accomplish this task, simply reviewing content in your target publications can be a great guide to identifying acceptable writing styles for editorial submissions.

Also check out the publication's editorial calendar for story ideas (often listed in their media kit or advertising section of their website). Knowing when to submit a story idea that fits into a topic that the publication is planning to cover is half the battle. Plan to get in touch with the editor at least 2-3 months before the topic is scheduled to inquire about submitting content.

PR Agency role: Social media management

PR Tool / Strategy: PR agencies have jumped onto the social media bandwagon in an attempt to position themselves as a necessary expert for managing social media activities for businesses. It is true they can certainly offer some good tricks of the trade and are often on the cutting-edge with new social media outlets, but any business can easily learn to manage their own social media presence to maximize their public relations exposure.

The social media outlets themselves are PR tools to utilize, but there are also social media dashboard and management resources to help businesses maximize their social media presence. See the Social Media section of this book for some specific strategies and tactics.

PR Agency role: Events and media inquiry management

PR Tool / Strategy: Big events typically require someone that can speak to the media on behalf of the company to communicate news and give or coordinate interviews. By establishing an event marketing process, your in-house team should be able to effectively manage extra PR tasks that may come along with special events.

Managing events is a particularly easy task if you only have a few events a year to focus on. General media inquiries can also be managed more effectively with a well-organized website press room (covered in this book) to help prioritize and respond to initial press needs.

Identifying Your In-House PR Potential

There is definitely an argument that can be made for establishing a relationship with a PR agency or PR consultant as a learning experience to get started.

Many small businesses have little to no experience in public relations and can use some extra guidance and expertise to get started. Even after thoroughly reading this book and investigating the resources and tools noted throughout, businesses may need a little extra hand-holding to jumpstart their public relations efforts (particularly start-ups with little PR exposure).

A PR agency can also be a good resource to help businesses define their public relations strategies and goals within a marketing plan. Providing an analysis of industry publications, events or other opportunities could be a good consulting task as well. If you are paying a PR agency or consultant to help you get started, choose time-consuming jobs that will result in tangible resources that you can use independently down the road.

After a period of time working with a PR agency, a business can then decide if they have learned enough to handle their public relations initiatives independently... or if they want to retain the help of an agency for certain aspects of their public relations activities that need extra support.

If your business is diving into new industries or geographic areas and you have no idea how to begin to develop a media outreach plan, consulting with a PR agency may be a good start.

PR agencies and PR professionals have access to media planning tools (usually subscription-based and too costly for the average small business) that they can use to identify publications and websites that meet your target audience. Their knowledge of how to effectively use these specialized tools can be a huge help. They can do a lot of the leg work necessary to get you started on developing an industry-specific PR strategy.

A business may also find that reaching out to media representatives for editorial coverage in print publications is too time-consuming or outside of their comfort zone.

PR agencies are experienced in pitching story ideas to publications and can even leverage existing media relationships that are developed from other client initiatives. Their writing staff can also be very helpful when asked to submit byline articles (fully written articles for inclusion in a publication). See Media Outreach chapter for more on that aspect.

Every Business is Unique

Of course every business has different public relations requirements, objectives and goals. In some cases not all of the typical PR agency roles may even be necessary to pursue (like writing editorial) for you to achieve your PR goals.

In other cases, the need for a particular public relations role (like media outreach or event management) may be so great that having additional assistance is needed to accomplish the task successfully. If this is the case, you may want to consider choosing between hiring a PR agency consultant (that is dedicated to PR tasks and activities) and hiring an additional person for your marketing staff that has the skills to multi-task with PR and other marketing needs.

Another exception for a need to hire a PR agency may be when a business is going through a major change – such as entering a new geographic area or country, going through an acquisition or launching a major new product initiative. Or, your business may be a start-up and you simply need help making the overall business launch successful.

These are times when outside help can extend the capabilities of your in-house marketing team to ensure that your new business ventures are as successful as possible. Investment in some professional PR help might be money well spent to give you the edge your business needs.

In the end, every business needs to assess their current business situation, priorities, staff skills, time capacity and budgets to determine if hiring an outside PR agency or consultant is a worthwhile investment.

Chapter 4: Determining Whether Company News Requires a Press Release

A press release is a great PR tool to get your message out to a large audience at a relatively low cost – and an obvious public relations medium for most businesses to pursue. It is usually the loudest way to toot your own horn when you want company news to be heard.

After a press release there is typically a spike in website traffic, customer inquiries and news coverage on websites and print publications. So of course most businesses like to issue press release on company news.

Sometimes every bit of news or company accomplishment may seem press-worthy in the eyes of the small business owner. But the truth is that not all company news requires a press release. At the same time, be sure to not overlook a press release opportunity for your business.

Here are some guidelines to consider that can help you avoid the problem of too much news or too little news released by businesses.

Too Much News

It is important to take a step back and determine whether company news really requires a formal press release or if another form of announcement (such as simply distributing website announcements through social media plugs) is more appropriate.

Businesses of any size need to be careful about penetrating the market with too many press releases because it can create "clutter" and overshadow real news opportunities that you want to communicate to the press, customers and potential partners.

Ask yourself the following questions when deciding whether your news is worthy of a press release:

- Is this news important information for my customers?

- Will announcing this news help my business acquire new customers, partners or investors?

- Is this news a significant development in my product line or ability to serve customers?

- Will this news be seen as innovative or game-changing within my industry?

There's also a cost consideration with press release distribution. Most press release services charge per release (unless you have signed up for some type of monthly or annual subscription). Sending out too many press releases is a good way to blow your budget – especially if the news is not newsworthy enough to bring about desired results.

Too Little News

Just as too much news can be seen as negative, having too little
news can make your company seem stagnant. Keeping a
constant flow of relevant and important news releases will
help keep your business on the radar with your customers and
in your industry.

Although there is not a suggested number or frequency for
distributing press releases, there are definitely times when
releasing news may be beneficial for your business.

News releases can be triggered or timed based on:

- major trade show or events for extra publicity

- seasonal industry peaks for sales boosts

- financial periods for investors (such as quarterly or end
of year)

Advantages of a Press Release

There are many obvious advantages of issuing a formal press
release – from increased news exposure to improving company
credibility.

A press release is a formal announcement of company news
and allows a business to control the presentation of the news
in a professional manner. The typical audience for a press
release is a member of an editorial team or journalist that
would cover the news in their publication or on their website.
This formal presentation of the news allows you to be able to
steer their editorial coverage by offering important details,
strategy insights, company spokesperson quotes and more.

Being the first to announce news that impacts major trends in
an industry can be a good way to influence your individual or

company credibility in an industry. Journalists are always looking for industry experts to reach out to for expertise, insights or general contribution to articles. Whether you are trying to position yourself as a thought-leader or your company's products or services as viable industry solution, the exposure you can get from press releases can have a definite impact on your credibility.

In today's internet world, the distribution of a press release also has a huge impact on overall company exposure and website traffic. Press releases properly optimized with relevant keywords will be picked up across many different outlets – including search engines, news wire sites, industry websites, trade publications and more (more on this in the SEO in Public Relations chapter).

Press release distribution services – along with recommended tools to use – will be covered more in the PR Distribution Services chapter of this book.

Press-worthy Company News Examples

With so many advantages associated with distributing a press release, over-announcing news is a very tempting possibility. Be sure that the news is actually substantial news for your company, industry or product segment.

Here are some examples of company news that warrants a press release:

- New product or service announcements

- Technological advancements (such as patents or software improvements)

- Expansion into a new market or geographic area

- Policy or service changes that benefit customers

- Major partnership or customer win announcements

- Awards, recognitions or industry accreditations

- Major company milestones (such as market share, number of locations, etc.)

- Company rebranding or management change

- Pre- or post-event announcements

- Financial announcements

Many businesses use their industry niche and/or geographic market as a guide to determine if news is press-worthy. Observe what is happening around you – in your market, industry or competitive space – and decide if your news is worthy of your target audience.

But remember –although competition can be a good gauge, just because your competition doesn't announce a certain type of news doesn't mean you shouldn't. Your competitors may not be as savvy with developing and distributing press releases. Plus, it is always good to stay ahead of the curve with your competition when it comes to public relations (or any marketing efforts) anyway.

Press Release Alternatives

So if your company news is not press release worthy (in other words, not big enough to justify a full press release), what are your options for getting the news out?

I like to put out "announcements" for news that seems worthy of an announcement, but not necessarily worthy of a full-blown press release. This is a good way to stretch your budget too.

Announcements can be in the form of a blog post or simply listed as "announcements" on a page of your website. Typically I write announcements in a slightly less formal style (although slightly more formal than a blog post because we are announcing something).

To help spread the word and get more visibility to these announcements, post them on your social media sites like Facebook, Twitter or LinkedIn. You can also forward them via email to your key media contacts for potential pick-up in their media and news coverage.

Finally, get more traction from announcements by posting them in your customer e-newsletters, promoting them in a news section on your company website home page or by elaborating on the news in a blog post feature story. By the way, these are all things that you can do and should do to promote press release activity as well.

Chapter 5: Press Release Writing Style and Format

A strong press release can be one of your most effective sales and marketing tools.

Announcing company news with a well-written press release that is professionally structured is essential to adequately communicate to media, partners, customers and potential business investors.

While press release writing styles tend to vary by business, industry, public relations professionals or simply personal writing styles, there are some basic elements that should be included in a standard press release.

By following a standard writing style and format for press releases, you can be sure that you frame up your news in a professional manner and include all relevant information for news and media targets.

Basic Components of Press Releases

A standard PR writing style and format for a company press release should include the following basic elements.

Headline. The headline is the most important element of a press release because it is most likely the line to be picked up by news outlets and catch attention of readers. Clearly state the company's news or announcement in one brief sentence (approximately 80 characters long) in a compelling way.

Examples:

> "XYZ Co. Announces the Launch of ABC Product for Managing Retail Products"

> "XYZ Co. Launches Redesigned Website with Online Services for Customers"

Subhead. The subhead elaborates on the headline and highlights key features or benefits of the release. The suggested length of the subhead is 1-2 sentences.

Examples:

> "ABC Product enables retailers to improve inventory management while reducing warehousing costs. Product uses cutting-edge logistics technology to help retailers compete better in their markets."

> "XYZ.com website gives customers the ability to customize products and manage orders with new streamlined account views and functionality."

Opening statement. The opening statement (or lead paragraph) of the press release introduces the key points of the release in a more concise announcement statement. Next to the title and subhead, the opening statement is one of most important elements of the press release because it is the summary most likely to be picked up by media.

Expansion of statement. The opening statement is typically followed by a broader or more detailed description of the news throughout the body of the release.

Company quote. It is always good to include a quote from an appropriate company executive offering a direct statement about why the company news is important to relevant targets of the release. Big news (such as a major partnership or financial news) should include a quote from the top company executive. If the news is focused on one area of the company, choose an executive best suited for presenting a quote (i.e. someone from marketing for new website or product, someone from customer service for service oriented news). Of course smaller businesses with limited staff may choose to use their top executive for all releases.

Summary statement. End the press release summarizing the news and offering forward statements about the next steps for the company or how the news may fit into other strategic initiatives.

Call to action (CTA). Every release should include some basic call to action statement that offers next steps for readers, such as a website, phone number or downloadable resource. What type of action do you want people to take after reading your release? Give them a "next step" that is actionable.

Company boilerplate copy. A standard corporate press release includes a concise, well-written company boiler copy – About XYZ Company – that provides an overview of the company products and services or mission.

Press ready resources. A good practice is to include downloadable resources that are press ready (high quality and available for immediate use in print or online) at the very end of a press release. These can include photos, images, charts or videos). Journalists will appreciate the availability of press ready resources because it will save them time and provide them with good visuals for their story coverage.

Contact information. Be sure to include the name, title and contact information (phone and email) for an appropriate company contact for inquiries. Depending on the size of your business this may be a marketing/PR person or the business owner. Typically the contact information is position at the very top of the release in the upper right or left under the header "Company Contact".

Special Considerations for a Strategic Partnership Press Release

A press release announcement of a new partnership should be structured to include essential agreement details that effectively launch the new relationship. Industry niche business publications and websites are likely to run coverage of a partnership press release when positioned as a strategic and influential business arrangement.

A strategic partnership press release includes all of the basic elements of a standard press release with some special considerations for the partnership.

Strategic partnership considerations include:

Headline. Headlines in partnership press releases are typically straight-forward announcing the two companies have formed a partnership. Sample headline: "XYZ Company and ABC Company Announce Strategic Partnership".

Subhead. The subhead elaborates on the extent of the partnership or the type of partnership that is formed. Sample subhead: "Partnership to include co-marketing of products and services with exclusive sales distribution".

Opening statement. The opening statement of the press release clearly states the new partnership agreement and restates the headline and subhead in a more concise announcement statement.

Expansion of statement. The opening statement is typically followed by a broader or more detailed description of the strategic agreement, further elaborating on the structure of the relationship.

Company quote #1 and #2. Partnership press releases should include a quote from both companies stating the importance of the new agreement and how it complements each company. A quote from the primary business in the partnership is listed first, followed by a quote from the secondary business. Sample quotes may include: "We are pleased to expand our relationship with XYZ Company" or "Our new partnership with ABC Company will help us expand into new markets".

Summary statement. Strategic partnership press releases should include a final summary that may offer a glimpse into how the partnership will be implemented, when customers will start seeing changes or other forward-thinking details.

Company boilerplate copy #1 and #2. A partnership release should include company boilerplate copy for each company. The primary company in the partnership or news is listed first.

Contact information. Be sure to include the name, title and contact information (phone and email) for appropriate company contacts for inquiries to either business. Depending on the size of your business this may be a marketing/PR person or the business owner. Again, the contact information is typically positioned at the very top of the release in the upper right or left under the header "Company Contact".

Tips for Creating a Good Press Release

In addition to identifying whether or not company news is worthy of a press release, businesses should first put together a sound strategy before beginning the press release writing process.

Take a step back to evaluate and outline key objectives of the release and what you hope to communicate with the news announcement. Then, set goals that you hope to accomplish with the news – such as increasing media or customer inquiries, driving more traffic to your website or gaining the attention of potential investors.

Properly outlining marketing objectives and goals for your news will help you stay on track when creating the press release draft. It makes the writing process easier if you have outlined a game plan, but the end result will also be much better.

Press Release Review and Approval Process

Aside from your public company website, a press release is one of the most visible forms of communication your company will distribute. Therefore, a thorough review process is crucial to protect your company reputation and brand.

A press release review process should include:

- **Proofreading review**. Have several people proofread the release for basic spelling or grammatical errors.

- **Marketing review**. Have your marketing communications or search marketing expert (if different from your in-house PR person) review the release for inclusion of relevant keywords for search engine optimization, as well as proper positioning of products or strategies within the market.

- **Legal review**. If your company has a legal consultant, a quick legal review is a good idea – particularly if you are announcing financial or major partnership information.

- **Customer/partner review**. Any third parties noted in the release have an opportunity to review and provide necessary edits. In many cases, a partnership release will require a full press release review while a customer may only need to approve their quote or input in the release.

- **Management review**. Make sure any senior managers in your company have a chance to review final drafts before release.

For more assistance in the press release creation, use the **Press Release Checklist** and the **Press Release Template** (developed by SBMarketingTools.com) to guide you through the process. The links to download these free bonus tools are located at the end of this book under the Directory of PR Marketing Tools chapter.

Chapter 6: Using SEO in Public Relations

With the emergence of social media and online press release distribution services, having press releases and public relations activities well-optimized for search engines is more important than ever.

If you are an online business then you already know how critical search engine optimization (SEO) can be for success. Your visibility in search engine results is dependent on using relevant keywords within the content of your site – and your business success is dependent on your website's visibility on search engines. But even if you don't have an online e-commerce business, your website visibility likely drives much of your business growth through inquiries.

Using relevant keywords in public relations activities (like press releases) is just as important to any business that desires online visibility from publicity (and really who doesn't?). Your PR efforts should include searchable terms that will help your company place better against the competition in search engine results. And each use of these keywords builds on your company's relevance within search engine results.

So when you put together a game plan for website search engine optimization (which hopefully you are already making a routine process for your business), be sure to include PR in your plans.

Optimizing PR Efforts with Keywords

Companies need to incorporate a SEO (search engine optimization) strategy with all of their marketing efforts – including public relations. Because any public relations activity can be used online, optimizing PR efforts with keywords is an important way to influence your company website ranking within search engines.

Here are some basic tips for optimizing keywords in public relations efforts:

> **Press releases**. Press releases properly optimized with relevant keywords can be a huge traffic producer for businesses. In fact, generating website traffic is one of the main reasons many businesses put out press releases.

> An emphasis should be placed in headlines and opening paragraphs, with other keywords used throughout the body. When appropriate, hyperlink keywords in your release to your website to create a relevant backlink to your site.

> **Articles and editorial coverage**. Although companies are often not able to control how they are mentioned in articles and editorial, they can still influence the use of keywords through prepared statements, backgrounders, quotes and press releases.

Using the right terminology will help ensure that your company will be referenced within context (and keywords) that is most beneficial for your business.

Company websites. Keywords should be generally optimized throughout websites (in content, page titles, page descriptions, metatags, etc.) regardless of PR efforts, but you want to be sure to also align website keyword optimization with any PR initiatives.

For example, landing pages associated with news should include the same relevant keywords you used in your press release. Also, including your keyword optimized press release in your website press room will help generate additional search traffic to your site. (See more on setting up a website press room later in this book).

Social media outreach. Use keywords in all social media outreach. Using keywords in hash tags in tweets (such as: #KEYWORD) is important to be searchable in Twitter, but also because tweets from twitter can be picked up by search engines... helping your company get even more exposure in search results.

Be sure to also pick important keywords that are trending for your industry. For example, if your news is related to an industry event, conference or trade show you'll want to use the hashtag for that event in your tweets (typically the acronym for the show is the one to use – check with the twitter account associated with the event to identify the hashtag to use).

Associating your tweet activity with an event that is being followed by using a hashtag can be a powerful tool to get more exposure for your business throughout an event period because people interested in that industry event will be closely following that hashtag.

Benefits of Online PR Coverage

In many cases, press releases will be broadly picked up by online news sites, publication websites, news feeds and search engines without ever making it to print.

While having print editorial on company news is certainly a home run in terms of public relations coverage, the more likely scenario will be online coverage. But that's OK. Get over the idea that being in print is better than online coverage. While the perceived prestige of print coverage may seem like the ultimate PR coup, online coverage of public relations activity can have many, many benefits over print.

Some benefits of online coverage include:

- **Timeliness of news**. New and editorial can be covered quickly and be more relevant than printed coverage that can become somewhat dated with long print publication cycles.

- **Website traffic**. Online coverage with links to a company website can be a great source of website traffic.

- **Keyword juice**. Hyperlinked keywords from a relevant site (known as back links) can be very beneficial to a company website ranking.

- **Long shelf life**. Online coverage is accessible on websites and by search engines for a much longer period of time than print coverage. The news or editorial coverage may continue to benefit your company for years.

- **Social sharing**. Online coverage can easily be extended through social networks through tweets, likes and shares to optimize the exposure of company news, editorial or other public relations activities.

Many press release distribution services offer "Search Engine Optimized" releases that help ensure that press releases are picked up by search engines. But it is really up to you to make sure that you are using proper keywords in your release in the first place in order for it to get noticed by search engines.

Don't Overdo Keywords and SEO

Be careful to not overdo your SEO practices throughout the keyword optimization process – overdoing your keywords is also known as keyword stuffing.

An overly keyword optimized release or website will actually harm your site with search engines (particularly with Google). Just write naturally and use words non-repetitively throughout your content that are relevant to your business and accurately communicate your message. Use relevant keywords in important places – like the headline, summary and conclusion – but use them sparingly and naturally.

Chapter 7: Press Release Distribution Strategies & Tools

There was a time when distributing a press release used to be a mysterious task that only public relations professionals seemed to be able to accomplish.

In fact, it actually really was a much more expensive and complicated task to send out a release "over the wire" that could be picked up by news organizations. But things have changed drastically in recent years.

Today there are numerous press release distribution tools available for small businesses to easily handle the task of distributing news in-house. Online press release distribution tools allow businesses of any size to upload a press release and have it widely distributed to online news sites, traditional news outlets, industry niche publications, local or regional media, search engines and more for a relatively low cost.

Now, any business can get professional news distribution services with a self-serve online tool.

Selecting the Best Press Release Distribution Tool

There are so many options for small businesses to release news the biggest problem seems to be choosing which press release distribution tool to use.

How do you choose the best tool to use for your business?

Each press release distribution tool offers some fairly standard services that are somewhat expected nowadays.

Some of the services you want to be sure you get when you sign-up with a press release distribution tool include:

- Distribution network to large network of offline and online news outlets

- Distribution network for all major search engines

- Targeting by industry and/or geography

- Ability to add links to your website

- Ability to embed links (use anchor text for keywords)

- Ability to include images, videos or files with the release

- Contact mechanisms to reach your company

- Company pages to track previous releases

- Hosted listing of news releases by category/industry

- Tracking and reports (impressions, reads, clicks/referrals)

Paid Press Release Distribution Tools

There are a lot of press release distribution tools that are available for businesses on a small budget to use.

Most of them offer varying levels of service (with varying levels of features and price points) that are available for use for one-time fees or prices. If you send out releases often, most will offer cost-effective subscription plans as well.

Here's a breakdown of some of the top press release distribution tools that I like for small businesses:

PRWeb – one of the most popular press release distribution tools, PRWeb.com is a very easy-to-use online tool that enables you to distribute and track press releases. Their basic press release distribution packages allow you to target industries and media outlets by geography (at the state and city level), as well as link to your website and upload images with press releases.

Your press release can receive a lot of web traffic directly from PRWeb's online categories by industry, as well as through search engines and online news outlets that pick up the release. Your small business is also in good company at PRWeb because it is widely used by Fortune 500 companies as well as small businesses.

eReleases – an popular press release distribution tool, eReleases.com has an exclusive partnership with PR Newswire, a Tier-1 news release organization that is typically used by large businesses to reach national publications.

Offering the same type of reach at a much lower cost, eReleases also features a database of over 100,000 subscribing journalists that receive press releases. With eReleases you also get the ability to target by industry, geography and get guaranteed inclusion on AP newswire.

24-7 Press Releases – offers a variety of press release distribution packages that are matched with the type of distribution you are seeking (an priced accordingly so you are not paying for more that you need).

Packages range from basic online visibility, to SEO and targeted media exposure to broad mass media coverage. They also have a free press release service that receives limited distribution.

For links to these press release distribution tools (along with the latest trial offers and deals) go to our PR Tool Directory:

http://www.sbmarketingtools.com/public-relations-tools

Free Press Release Distribution Tools

There are also a lot of "free" options for press release distribution that are worth taking advantage of if you have little to no budget.

Of course the old mantra "you get what you paid for" is certainly the case when using free services. Distribution is limited, tracking is limited or not available at all and your press release will most likely run next to advertising for other products and services (that could also be advertising your competitors).

But if your budget is really tight, taking advantage of a free press release distribution service may be better than doing nothing at all.

Some press release distribution tools that offer a free service:

www.PR.com

www.PRlog.org

www.free-press-release.com

www.i-newswire.com

www.express-press-release.net

www.1888pressrelease.com

Watch for Hidden Costs and Add-ons

Most of the press release services will lure you in with a low teaser rate. While you can certainly send out a press release at that low rate, they'll often try to up-sell you on other services. These additional services could be editorial review, premium placement in their listings, extra distribution outlets and more.

Most of these services that can be tacked onto the base press release distribution services are not necessary. So don't assume that you have to add on additional services and costs when you put out a release. Obviously, if you feel that your company needs the extra help then take advantage of the services if needed.

Choosing the Best PR Distribution Tool for Your Business

Using a free distribution service may be a good way to test the waters with press releases (especially if you have little to no budget). Note that if you decide to use a free press release service they also offer a paid service that will give you more distribution and exposure. You could choose to use their free service first and then decide if you want to increase exposure for future releases go with a paid upgrade or another paid service. It would be a good way to test how much bang you get for your extra buck if you use a free service one time and then a paid service another time.

But honestly my preference for big news is to use a trustworthy paid service that you know will get your company noticed. Which service does your competitor use, or is most used within your industry niche? How well does the service seem to categorize relevant news?

For example, I liked that PRWeb actually had a specific category for marine/boating for my client in the boating industry. When I checked them out I also noticed that there were many relevant companies from the boating industry that appeared under that category. This told me that it was a reputable source for many other companies in the industry and that having press releases listed in a specific online category for our target industry would likely provide more exposure. For what it's worth, we have been using PRWeb for several years now and are very pleased.

Of course different people like different features, so I always recommend trying more than one tool to see what works best for you. For some, ease-of-use is the most important factor, while others it really just comes down to cost.

Chapter 8: Media Outreach and Building Key Media Relationships

A targeted media outreach plan should be part of every public relations strategy when launching a company press release or attempting to secure editorial coverage.

Often companies send out a press release via traditional mass press release distribution channels and become disappointed when media coverage is lacking in targeted publications. You may wonder: Why didn't they pick it up?

Well, for one, editorial teams for online or print publications are very limited in staff these days and become swamped with a plethora of news each day. Sometimes it's just hard to cut through the daily clutter.

Another potential reason: they just didn't get it. Yes, they got the release... but they didn't get [understand] what it really meant. Sometimes journalists need clarification on why the news is important for them to cover for their audience.

Many businesses make the mistake of just putting out a press release and expecting the traffic and media inquiries or pickups to automatically follow. Sometimes it does, but most of the time you will need to put a little more effort into generating the maximum amount of media exposure from your press releases.

Implementing some thoughtful strategies to help your press release, media alert or company news stand out in a news cycle is critical to ensure adequate media coverage in the targeted publications that are most important to your business.

Here are some PR marketing tips for getting more and better media coverage for your business.

Develop a Key Targeted Media List for Press Releases

Simply blasting out a press release to all available media outlets within an industry or geographic area is not an effective way to ensure media coverage. Although distribution of a press release to a full targeted media list is important, a key targeted media list (or short list) of the most important publications should be developed and nurtured.

Knowing which publications are the best fit for your niche industry should be the number one goal for more media exposure. Develop a list of the media outlets targeted for your industry based on important criteria like their target audience, geographic distribution and editorial focus. If appropriate, create segments for different types of news coverage you may want to achieve in your target industry.

This short list of key targeted media publications should be the primary publications that are most influential in your niche industry or target audience. These publications (online or print) are typically involved in trade organizations (or even run by trade organizations), publish in-depth articles and news reports and cater to a valuable demographic or audience.

Ask yourself – what are the must-read publications in my industry? There may be only one or two, or there may be as many as three or four important publications. Put these publications at the top of your key targeted media list for future outreach when seeking press release media coverage.

Define PR Strategies for Targeted Publications

Understanding the specific business angles each targeted publication seeks to cover in their publications is a good strategy when trying to get media coverage of press releases. Stay up to date on the type of coverage the publications provides on their website and/or print publication.

For example, if the publication is more focused on strategic business announcements (as opposed to product-focused announcements) make sure you plan to stress the strategic significance of your press release announcement – within your press release as well as in your pre-launch media alerts.

Establish Relationships with Editors and Editorial Representatives

Knowing which publications (print or online) are most influential for your business is only half the battle. You need to also get to know the individual contacts that control media coverage.

Be sure to proactively reach out to media contacts – particularly for your key targeted media – and introduce them to your company prior to hitting them with press releases and asking for coverage. Start an open dialogue with the editorial representatives (editors, writers or other editorial team members) so they have a baseline for your business.

Often there are multiple contacts that serve different editorial roles within a media outlet. You should make note of who is in charge of what to help streamline potential coverage.

For example, there may be one person that simply handles picking up and running press releases. Although often not the most influential media contact for major editorial stories within a publication, these contacts can be very important for ensuring your press releases are included in daily coverage of news and get proper exposure.

If press release coverage is a big concern, reach out to the editorial contact in charge of running release coverage and learn their process.

- Do you need to get them an advance copy before 3:00 pm in order it in their morning news coverage?

- Do they prefer a media alert summary in addition to the full release?

- Do they prefer the content in word as opposed to a PDF?

- Are press ready photos required?

They'll appreciate your outreach to make their job easier, and the result will be more consistent and timely coverage of your press releases. As you work with different editorial contacts you will learn what their preferences are – sometimes they will simply tell you if you ask, other times it is a learning curve after dealing with them over a period of time.

Providing editors and editorial representatives with things like a company overview, strategic business highlights and a synopsis of your influence within the relevant industry niche will make them more receptive to your press release announcements. Any media coverage of company news is also likely to be more thorough.

Finally, be sure to thank everyone for the coverage. Be friendly in your requests, show respect and appreciation... it can go a long way in building a mutually beneficial relationship!

Position You or Your Company as an Industry Expert

One of the best tactics or strategies to ensure more media exposure is positioning you and your company as a thought leader and go-to industry expert. Most journalists will tell you that expertise is one of the most important factors when seeking a contributor to a news or feature story.

When industry publications are working on industry stories, articles or coverage of industry news they often seek out industry experts for their insight. Many small businesses already have someone in their business that has a deep level of expertise because that expertise is how the business got started in the first place. The company itself may offer specialized services or expertise that can also be seen as innovative within the industry.

Don't be shy about making it known within your industry what value you bring to the discussion. Give your individual business experts as much exposure as you can through your website, blog, forums and on social media so that the word gets out about your expertise.

Being active on niche blogs outside of your business is also very helpful to establish expertise within your industry.

Finally, be sure you **pitch** your expertise to your target media contact list to let them know that you are available for exclusive interviews and contributions to editorial coverage as needed.

Some publications will also accept matte releases or byline articles which are fully written articles for their publications. If the author is well-known and respected in the industry these are generally very welcomed by publishers. Be sure to pitch the story or article idea to the editor for consideration before spending time writing the article.

Send Pre-Launch Media Alerts of Press Releases

Editors like to feel like they are given an opportunity for a scoop on developing industry news. A pre-launch media alert or media advisory (a.k.a. advance notice) of a press release can be sent to your key targeted media contacts and journalists to let them know you are giving them an opportunity for media coverage prior to a full public announcement or distribution.

This can be a good tactic to ensure media coverage with your top publication. If they think you are giving them an opportunity for something exclusive they may be more likely to cover the news.

Consider offering bonus extras like interviews with you, your top executives or key customers.

Provide Media with Press-Ready Images and Resources with Press Releases

Make it easy for media representatives to provide thorough coverage of your press release. One of the best PR tactics for getting media coverage is providing press-ready images or other resources that can be included within editorial coverage.

These press-ready images and resources could include:

- Photos

- Videos

- Charts or graphs

- Illustrations or diagrams

- Executive headshots (if applicable to release)

Press-ready images and resources should be noted as a directly downloadable link at the end of the release or in the pre-launch media alert with a description and/or caption. Make sure they truly are press-ready; meaning, they are quality high resolution images that require no touch-up for press usage (web or print).

Social Sharing and Publicity of Media Coverage

When you do get media coverage of a press release, make sure you are sharing the news coverage in social media outlets (such as LinkedIn, Twitter or Facebook) as well as your company blog or website.

Sharing the editorial coverage of your press release has several advantages. Of course, spreading the news first and foremost helps generate more exposure for your press release. But publication will also appreciate the extra publicity for their publication.

If publications are monitoring their website traffic and analyzing news popular news coverage they will see that your company's press release news coverage was well received and may be even more receptive to covering future press releases in their publication.

Specific strategies and tactics for Social Media PR are covered in the next chapter. To help you develop and track strategies with your media contacts, download our free bonus PR tool – **Media Outreach Guide** – at the end of this book under the Directory of PR Tools chapter.

Chapter 9: Using Social Media as part of a PR Strategy

Using social media networks like LinkedIn, Facebook, Twitter and Google+ can complement an overall PR plan, but should not replace good public relations techniques.

The public relations industry has seen a boost in free or low cost avenues for sharing company news with the spread of social media networks. Companies large and small are taking advantage of the platforms to announce news and start conversations about their products or services.

While an integrated social media plan is an important element of today's PR strategies, companies need to be careful not to rely entirely on publicizing news on social networks.

I've seen a lot of businesses try to substitute long-standing PR techniques – like press releases or media outreach – with simply blasting news and activity on all their social media sites.

Social media public relations require a balance between new and old PR tactics and techniques.

Pitfalls of Using Social Media Public Relations as a PR Replacement

Experienced public relations managers (or marketing managers) know never to rely on one tactic to produce results. Although social media public relations tactics can be highly effective and cost-efficient, a social network is not likely to meet all of a company's PR objectives.

When developing a social media public relations strategy, be careful of the potential pitfalls of using it as a replacement for traditional PR techniques.

- **Limiting direct contact with media**. Simply promoting company news and stories through social media can limit your ability to build valuable one-on-one relationships. Establishing good relationships with media representatives and journalists is important to land editorial coverage beyond a press release pick-up.

- **Avoiding press release distribution services**. Releasing company news via LinkedIn, Facebook or Twitter without releasing news using more formal PR distribution services can reduce the circulation of news to other online or print media. Press releases will get much wider distribution when they are released to media outlets typically covered by PR distribution services that journalists and news sites actively monitor.

- **Oversaturation of networks with company promotions**. Because social media networks are easy and free to use, connections can quickly feel oversaturated with PR communications and messages. There tends to be a lot of clutter on sites like Twitter or LinkedIn and, depending on your industry niche, it can be difficult to stand out. Also remember that social media is more effective if it is used as an interaction tool with back and forth communications.

Best Social Media Public Relations Tools

The top social media networks for supporting public relations strategies include LinkedIn, Facebook, Google+ and Twitter. These networks are the most widely developed and adopted social platforms with easy-to-use tools for small businesses.

Social media sites are also free marketing tools for businesses to leverage that only take an investment of time. Time is the biggest obstacle for most businesses struggling to learn how to use them effectively. It will take some time to establish a good base of LinkedIn business connections, Facebook Business Page likes or Twitter followers. To be most relevant, be sure that you are establishing social media connections that are specific to your business or industry.

In addition to the big players, each industry niche may also have other social networks that are relevant and worth checking out. To build a good base of social media sites specific to your business or industry niche, be sure to look into targeted industry blogs, website forums or other niche social sharing sites. Industry associations often have membership forums for specific segments – such as technology or retail – that can be highly targeted for your key audience and become a great social sharing tool for your business.

There are also other resources specifically for the small business segment that have a social element and are worth checking out. For example, BizSugar.com is a great resource to find useful and relevant information for small businesses from marketing to human resources to technology. The site is devoted to sharing news, resources and tips for small businesses. Members vote on each news item submitted so that really valuable resources easily go to the top of the list. Bizsugar can be especially valuable if you offer professional services for other small businesses.

Integrating Social Media Networks into PR Strategies

As we said, social media should not be a substitute for PR. You want to develop a PR strategy that utilizes social media networks as a marketing tool, rather than simply a one-way communication platform.

You want to also fully integrate social media connections into your public relations efforts so that they are complementary and work together toward the same goals and objectives.

Step One: Make Relevant Connections

When you expand your social media connections make sure they are relevant. Focus on people and businesses that compliment your business and industry so that when you share news on social networks it has the biggest benefit to your business.

Be sure to also focus on media and journalists you're your connections. Every business is looking to expand their social reach, and media outlets are no exception. Be sure to connect with media contacts and publications wherever they are on social media – Twitter, Facebook, Google+, LinkedIn and even on Pinterest.

Step Two: Engage Contacts

After you connect, be sure to engage frequently with your social contacts. The goal is to constantly remind them that you are a valuable business within your target industry. Be sure to stay active with their posts through comments, likes and shares (HINT: the more you like, comment or share with others, the more they are likely to do the same for you!)

Of course you want to be sure to also actively manage your social media accounts with a good flow of relevant content and posts. Use social media to communicate and engage network connections with relevant industry news and happenings through discussions. Social media networks are great tools to create viral buzz about a company. Try to engage connections by eliciting discussions, comments, likes, tweets, retweets, shares and other social media interactions.

Step Three: Integrate Social with PR Activity

Most press release distribution tools now feed new releases directly to your linked social media accounts. This can be a real time-saver and also ensure that your news is distributed and integrated with your social media accounts each time you have news.

All of the above social media public relations activity should be on top of traditional PR marketing tactics and techniques. The combined effort will grow your company's buzz and recognition further than single, unsupported PR strategies and efforts.

More specific strategies for social media networks are covered in the next chapter on Social Media Strategies and Tactics.

Chapter 10: Strategies and Tactics for Social Media Sites

Social media sites are definitely the best free communication tool that small businesses have at their disposal for public relations. And as we mentioned, social media can be a valuable enhancement to your traditional public relations activities.

Each of the major social media sites have a similar theme – share information (news, opinions, ideas, photos, videos and more) with a networked connection of contacts.

But how you use each social media site can be quite different – from identifying connections to communicating and sharing information to get the word out about your business. Each site may also have a different purpose or target audience for your business. For example – you may find LinkedIn to be a good outlet for reaching industry contacts, but Facebook is a great way to connect with customers and build buzz with them.

Here are some more specific strategies and tactics for leveraging some of the top social media sites for the purposes of creating buzz, visibility and exposure for your business.

YouTube Videos

YouTube videos are my favorite way to create PR buzz... and they tend to be under-utilized in many industries. Posting a video on YouTube is one of the easiest and most interactive ways to reach the masses with your message.

A basic YouTube video brand channel is free to set-up and video PR messages can be used for company announcements, product or service promotions or partnership press releases. Videos can be embedded into websites or blogs (to help make sites more interactive), as well as shared across your other social media sites. With the proper use of keywords in your video title, description and tags, your videos can generate even more views from organic search engine results, YouTube searches and related videos on YouTube.

With a basic video camera, any company can easily create a library of videos to promote their business.

Some ideas for using YouTube videos as a PR marketing tool include:

- Product promotional videos

- Trade or industry event preview or recap videos

- Company executive interview videos

- Customer testimonial videos

- New product or service offering announcement videos

- New partnership announcement videos

- Photo collage videos highlighting key messages, products, projects or other accomplishments

Using a brand channel on YouTube gives businesses the ability to create a mini-site within YouTube to organize and showcase PR videos. Traffic can be measured and monitored through YouTube analytics to understand traffic sources and overall reach of public relations videos. With proper use of keywords in video descriptions, YouTube videos can generate traffic beyond typical traffic sources.

YouTube videos are typically accessed by organic search engine results , YouTube video search results, related video recommendations on YouTube and direct links from company websites. Many press release distribution tools also allow you to use video in your actual press release.

The reach of videos is further extended through social media sharing. Links to YouTube videos are often shared on Twitter or embedded on Facebook. The viral marketing effect of sharing videos can be a huge help to public relations efforts.

LinkedIn

LinkedIn has quickly become the best social media site for professional networks. When you remain active on LinkedIn your professional connections and groups will then be more receptive to news releases, product updates and other PR announcements.

Here are some specific strategies to get the most out of your PR presence on LinkedIn:

- **Personal Profile:** Create a clear and detailed personal profile that clearly articulates your business, background experience and skills. This will help with establishing your expertise credentials for media contacts as well as expanding your network of professional connections.

- **Network Connections**: Maintain a good network of professionals and media representatives to get the word out within your niche industry.

- **Status Updates:** Be sure to use the status update functionality on LinkedIn to post frequent updates about your business. Status updates are visible in the activity stream of your contacts. Select the Twitter box with a status update to automatically tweet to your connected Twitter account.

- **Groups**: Being a member of relevant industry groups on LinkedIn as an active participant in discussions is very important to keep you and your company top of mind. Groups are also a good place to post news and information about your business. You can also create your own group on LinkedIn for any topic. Managing a LinkedIn group gives you the opportunity to self-promote by sending out announcements to group members (although it is recommended to use this feature sparingly) and setting up RSS feeds from your blog and/or press releases.

- **Company Pages**: Make sure your company profile page is very thorough and updated often with product information highlights. LinkedIn has expanded their company pages to include much more than job postings (a feature that many small businesses may not be able to tap into). In addition to a company overview you can have a product page with images, product descriptions, video embeds and links to your website. The main page for your company page now gives you the option of a header and promoting company news through posts that people following your company will see in their news feeds.

Facebook

Maintaining a Facebook business page is another great PR tool
– particularly for businesses that market to consumers.
Facebook can be a great way to generate buzz and interest for
your brand. Facebook can also have a viral effect with "likes"
and comments that can be seen by friends of friends to
improve your publicity potential. Your loyal fans are some of
your best brand advocates, so use Facebook wisely if you have
a strong following.

Facebook has become somewhat challenging for small
businesses with the introduction of something called
"EdgeRank". Basically Facebook no longer shows ALL of your
fans ALL of your posts anymore. In fact, only about 25% of
your fan base actually sees your posts unless you pay to
"promote posts". So depending on how big your fan base is, it
could cost $5, $10, $20 or more to reach 100% of your fans by
promoting a post.

There are also other tools like "Offers" that are special
discounts offers you can set and generate additional exposure
for your business when fans claim them (their friends will see
claimed offers in their news feed). The "Events" feature is
actually free and can be a good way to publicize and invite fans
to special company events.

So this once free tool is no longer entirely free for businesses,
but it can still be a very cost-effective way to engage and
promote your business to an interested audience. If you are
willing to invest a little bit of money, Facebook advertising
campaigns and promoted posts can help get your company
extra publicity and extend your PR reach.

From a search engine standpoint, Facebook activity is
currently integrated with Bing search results. The pages or
websites that your fans "like" are visible in the sidebar of Bing
and may influence search traffic. Although the use of Bing is a

fraction of the search market compared to Google, it can be helpful for additional visibility within search results for your news related posts on Facebook.

Twitter

Most people either love or hate Twitter. If you love it, then you probably understand how to use it. If you hate it, then you may just not understand how to tap into its full potential when it comes to publicizing your business.

Twitter should be used to help extend the reach of news, as well as make connections with individuals and businesses within your industry. Using the right hash tags (or keywords preceded by the # sign) is critical to success with Twitter.

When you send out a "tweet" (also known as a status update on other social site) you can promote news along with a website link, photo and special hash tags that people help people find your tweet (all within 140 characters, which can get tricky!).

If your key media contacts follow certain hash tags, then make sure you use them in your tweets. As mentioned earlier in the SEO chapter, find out what hash tags are important to your industry and be sure to use them. For example, if there is a big trade industry event that everyone is following on Twitter you want to use the hash tag for the event (such as **#XYZSHOW**) to make your tweet visible with that event.

Also take advantage of tweeting pictures and links to videos to make your news tweets more interactive, engaging and re-tweet-worthy. Like Facebook, you can invest money in important news through promoted tweets and other advertising to extend your media reach. This can be a worthwhile feature to explore when you have really big news to share with a targeted audience.

Google+

In 2012 Google jumped into the social media game with the introduction of Google+. While the same basic functionality as other social networks exists with Google+ (such as making connections, posting status updates, commenting and sharing), the ability to create "circles" on Google Plus is a targeting functionality that is unique.

Google+ circles gives businesses more control over posts and status updates by giving them the ability to better define who receives communications. Circles – if created with the right strategy in mind – can effectively turn this social network tool into a direct marketing or news generation tool for businesses to promote products and services to specific audiences.

Google+ also offers additional social tools such as Events and Google+ communities that resemble LinkedIn Groups. Their video chat functionality known as "Hangouts" is unique to the other social platforms and has interesting PR potential for company announcements and such.

Google+ is still a growing platform and is likely to be much less cluttered for your industry. This gives you the opportunity to stand out and get noticed by journalists and key industry professionals that are already on board. Personally I find that it is much easier to cut through the clutter on Google+ and engage in exchanges with targeted contacts. Of course this may change as the network and use grows.

One final word about Google+... it is definitely worthwhile to develop a broad network of connections because of the potential influence on your Google search ranking. Google gives preferential treatment in search results from people in your Google+ circles or websites you have given a "+1" when the "Show Personal Results" tab is selected (a default option by the way). This integration is similar to the Bing and Facebook integration, but Google is obviously much more widely used for searches. So developing a large network of people who +1 your website or Google+ posts may become a good traffic generator for you in the future.

Pinterest

Pinterest has quickly become a social media sharing phenomenon and is worth mentioning for future PR potential. Small businesses with a highly visual product offering (think retail products) can really make a name for their brand by having images or videos shared on Pinterest.

If you are not familiar with Pinterest yet, you better get up to speed fast if you fit into the retail or visual product category.

Basically Pinterest is like a virtual corkboard where users can "pin" images they find online to boards with a general theme. The biggest demographic on Pinterest is women, and boards associated with things like decorating, wedding planning, kids, cooking and the like tend to be hot topics.

The biggest advantage for business brands is that images "pinned" from your website maintain a link back to the original source on your website... so it can become a big traffic generator for your business.

You can improve your chances of getting "pinned" on Pinterest by creating buzz-worthy images of your products, using large "pin-friendly images" on your website (about 600 pixels wide is best) and having a "pin it" badge under images on your website. Even if you don't have retail-oriented products you can create infographics or other interesting images that can be shared on Pinterest.

Blogs, Forums or Websites

Don't forget about tapping into other industry blogs, forums or websites as a method to get your news out to your niche industry. Establish connections with these sites and try sending a press release or product news announcement directly to the blog or website requesting PR coverage or a story write-up.

Offering pre-written content with press-ready photos is also very helpful to make website or blog coverage easier. Many smaller blogs are very eager to generate new content and would be happy to run a guest blog post if it is not too self-serving (but do ask for a brief author bio with link to your website at the end).

If you are able to get a guest post segment with a larger blog or website that has a large audience it can be very lucrative for your website traffic. More importantly, creating authority and expertise for you or your business has many PR benefits. Most of these larger sites will require a commitment of ongoing submissions, so be prepared to generate content for them.

With forums, identify websites that maintain a highly trafficked forum with a relevant audience or topic. Get social with these forums by posted on relevant topics often and occasionally plugging your news (without spamming them of course). Forums that allow a website link in your posts and in your signature will give you the best exposure.

Chapter 11: Local PR Strategies and Tactics

As small towns everywhere work hard to recover from a global recession, there is a reinvigoration around the idea of patronizing local businesses to help local economies.

The good news is that this "shop small, buy local" trend is very uplifting to small businesses that depend on their loyal, local customers to keep their businesses running and profitable.

If you run a local small business, you'll want to take advantage of a revived focus on **shopping locally** and work that theme into your local PR efforts (as well as your local marketing efforts in general).

The "local angle" is also very well received by local media that are interested in highlighting businesses that have a positive impact on local communities... by offering a local service, creating jobs or giving back to the community. Embracing your business impact or contribution to your local community can be a great PR strategy.

Defining a Local PR Plan

Many of the same basic strategies for your overall PR plans apply to a local plan, but a more targeted approach for your specific community opportunities is required. Your local PR plan may include enhancements like:

> **Messaging** – you'll want to create a local pitch, focusing your message on what you offer your local community. Does supporting your business support local economic growth? Maybe it supports local farmers or manufacturers? Emphasize the number of years you have been providing services to a community, your dedication to local customers and partners and your commitment to growing your local economy.

> **Targeted Media** – local media exposure typically extends beyond industry trade to more mainstream local TV, community newspapers, magazines and websites. While more mainstream local media may not be as interested in advancements within your industry they will be interested in your impact or offering within the local community. Be sure to present your local message in a compelling manner for each targeted media segment.

> **Charity and community support** – charities play a big part in local PR efforts – contributing to local causes in terms of time, money or in-kind services/products is a worthwhile effort. Being a good company makes you a great company. Make an ongoing effort to support the local charities or causes (such as schools, community centers, churches, etc.) that are important to your business and community.

Local PR and Marketing Events

Creating or participating in a local event is as much of a PR opportunity as it is a marketing opportunity for your business. Your participation gives you the opportunity to send out press releases, offer company interviews, contribute to event news coverage and amp up exposure within your local market.

Local PR and marketing event opportunities can include things like:

- Product or service launches

- New store or location grand openings

- Company milestone celebration (10 of years in business, 1,000th customer served, 1 millionth widget made, etc.)

- Ribbon cutting ceremonies on project completions

- Charitable donation presentations

- Sponsorships at charitable fundraisers (such as walks, marathons or donation drives)

- Book signings with authors

- Local celebrity appearances

- Special sales or giveaway events

- Fun competitions or customer participation events

Each local event will be unique to your business, your community and media opportunities, but here are some tips to help your local PR events more successful:

- Create a "real" event and be careful your event is not seen as just a PR or publicity stunt.

- Send out media advisories or alerts that give local media outlets a compelling reason to attend.

- Contact big media outlets like local TV stations, radio stations and newspapers as well as smaller niche media outlets like local news websites, community newspapers or smaller radio stations (like college or university stations)

- Ask partners, customers, suppliers or local associations to help spread the news and create buzz for optimal attendance and post-event coverage

- Follow-up with media outlets supplying additional photos, video clips and detailed reports for potential coverage – even if they didn't make the event they may make use of it

Small Business Saturday Promotion

A growing local business marketing and PR opportunity is **Small Business Saturday**. Businesses have a new annual marketing and PR opportunity with the 2010 launch of Small Business Saturday in the U.S. Nestled between Black Friday (the Friday after Thanksgiving) and Cyber Monday (the Monday after Thanksgiving), Small Business Saturday is aimed at supporting retail sales for local small businesses and merchants.

Thanks to American Express and other small business supporters, a new day has been created specifically for promoting neighborhood businesses so that they can benefit from a surge of retail business over the busy Thanksgiving weekend shopping time period.

The goal of Small Business Saturday organizers is to promote consumer patronage of neighborhood merchants, retailers and local neighborhood shops. With so much attention given to big retailers and discount super stores for Black Friday and Cyber Monday deals over Thanksgiving weekend, the effort hopes to shift focus to small businesses.

There are many small local merchants struggling to compete against bigger businesses, and the Small Business Saturday event hopes to put an annual focus shopping with local retailers and merchants on Thanksgiving weekend nationwide.

With the backing of a major small business supporter such as American Express, the event continues to get a big boost in local and national media. Local retailers and merchants should plan to use Small Business Saturday as an important part of their overall local marketing and PR efforts each year... **and throughout the year**.

Here are some strategies for incorporating Small Business Saturday into a holiday marketing and PR plan:

> **Increase exposure on social media**. Participate in American Express sales promotions on Facebook and other social media sites. Be sure to ramp up your overall social media exposure in the weeks leading up to Small Business Saturday and encourage participation at your store location(s).

> **Promote sales incentives**. Be sure your customers and prospects are aware of the special incentives offered on Small Business Saturday through American Express or

any other participating organizations. Add signs at your store and information on your web site.

Plan additional sales events. Increase the incentives with special one-day discounts and promotions that will improve foot traffic into your store location.

Build communication database. Use the Small Business Saturday event as an opportunity to build your own customer database for email marketing or direct mail to continue to communicate to local consumers about special retail shopping events throughout the year.

The Small Business Saturday event is a great example of how you can leverage your presence in a local community (and the fact that you are a small business) to create more awareness and a positive public perception locally. In essence, turn the fact that you are a small local business into a differentiator that sets your business apart from bigger businesses.

Chapter 12: Building and Managing a Website Media Press Room

A press room is an essential content component of any company website. Many big businesses use website press rooms, and there is no reason why small businesses should overlook the opportunity to formally present their company press essentials with one.

The main purpose of a website press room is to give journalists and media representatives vital company information for feature editorials and media coverage.

Much of the content in a website press room is comparable to a press kit (company backgrounder, executive bios, releases, etc.). But a website press room is also an opportunity for companies to promote recent accomplishments and communicate a company vision to media, customers, prospects and potential investors.

Most importantly, a well-organized and up-to-date website press room will help ensure that it fully supports your PR goals and objectives for media coverage and proper company representation.

Tips for Website Press Room PR Content

Here are some tips for setting up a website press room to organize your press releases and other PR support content.

Press releases. A company website press room should include all recent press releases or company announcements, preferably organized in a descending date order with the most recent new release listed first.

Typically, a press room has a summary of press release titles that click through to web pages that contain the remaining content of the news release. If you have press-ready resources (such as photos, charts or videos), be sure to include links to download or embed resources.

Company overview. Media representatives expect to see general company boiler copy as well as company backgrounder content in a website press room. A basic overview of the line of products or services is often included in the company overview along with a general vision or mission statement.

Executive bios. Information about key company executives is good for potential press interviews. Include a professional headshot, relevant experience, credentials or accreditations of individuals that are most influential in your business.

Press coverage. A website press room is a good place to showcase previous news coverage and feature stories in publications. Add links to online media coverage, videos or link to a PDF reprint of print publication coverage. Most publications will require permission for online reprints but welcome the additional exposure to their publications.

Investor information. If your company is public, or seeking private equity investment, basic investor relations information should be included in a website press room with any investor-specific company contacts.

Most small businesses are actively seeking financial investments to help grow their company. If this is the case for your business, use your press room as an opportunity to promote any special investment opportunities you may be exploring, such as partnerships, distribution agreements, affiliates or private equity investments.

Contact information. Be sure to include contact information for key company contacts for media inquiries and executive interview requests. Set up a contact form or having an email address specific for media inquiries that is different than your typical contact form for sales inquiries.

New Public Relations Content Ideas for Press Rooms

Companies can make their website press room even more valuable to media representatives, investors and customers with additional public relations content ideas that provide value-added company news information.

Personally, I think you only risk missing out on opportunities by having too little information in your press room. It never hurts to add just a little bit more than expected.

Expanding basic website press room PR content with new and innovative ideas will give media representatives the tools needed to effectively cover company news. And a good media press room is also a good way to impress customers and prospects with credentials and accomplishments, improving sales opportunities and customer loyalty.

New public relations content ideas for website press rooms include:

Press Ready Images - Offer downloadable, press-ready images with press releases to make it easy for media representatives to cover company news online or in print. An archive of general press ready images (such as company logos or standard product photos) can also be made available for general media coverage opportunities. Journalists are more likely to cover a business when they can get quick and easy access to supporting images.

Social Media Feeds – Leverage your social media accounts and presence by having links to social media sites or a feed of recent Twitter tweets or Facebook posts. Twitter also has an "Embed this Tweet" feature that allows you to easily showcase favorable tweets on your website.

Blog Highlights – You spend a lot of time generating interesting content pieces for your blog and highlighting company blog posts is another great content sources that can generate media interest. Often blog posts elaborate on a topic that shows your company expertise and can help build your credibility for a specific topic. Company blogs can be a great showcase for media representatives (in addition to your customers, prospects or company partners).

Partnerships and Associations - Providing
information on key partners and associations can help
to highlight a company's important accreditations, as
well as elaborate on partnership news or
accomplishments.

Video Showcases – The use of video is an effective way
to promote and communicate company products,
services or mission statements. You can easily embed
company YouTube videos, as well as link to your
company's video channel on YouTube to add more
interaction with your website press room. Also include
links to any video or news coverage of your company.

Be sure to keep content in your website media press room
fresh, accurate and up-to-date so that it is both informative and
helpful for website visitors. Out of date information can be a
big turn-off to journalists and media representatives in search
of timely and thorough information.

Chapter 13: Maintaining a Public Relations Pipeline

As a small business owner your job is never done... and unfortunately the job of managing your own PR is also never done.

To keep your business top of mind with media, customers and prospects you'll want to constantly be thinking... what's my next move?

Of course this is not a new idea when it comes to running a business. You know the saying... you can't rest on your laurels of recent accomplishments and business wins... you always want to be striving for the next big one. With PR, you want to keep the news coming, keep the buzz flowing. You need to develop a pipeline of PR initiatives that will keep momentum going for your business.

It also helps to plan ahead so that you don't miss out on any PR opportunities that may come your way. While some public relations activities are reactive (particularly when it comes to mitigating potential negative PR situations), it is best to be as proactive as possible.

Using Customer Testimonials to Build a PR Pipeline

Simply creating goals can help you build a pipeline. And setting goals associated with something attainable, such as customer testimonials, will help build your PR pipeline AND help generate more sales.

Acquiring more customer testimonials is a great PR goal you can set for your business and strive toward throughout the year. How you quantify our specific goal should depend on your ability to get good testimonials (or even the number of customers you typically can reach throughout the year). For example, a reasonable goal for your business may be to acquire one new testimonial per month or quarter.

How do you get customer testimonials? The best way is to simply ask for them. When you know a customer is really happy with your product or service, ask them if they would be able to share their story with others. If you have an online transactional business, make it part of your online sales process to ask them to submit brief testimonials if they are pleased with their online experience.

Once you have a new customer testimonial you should have a set of PR tactics associated with promoting it.

PR tactics to promote customer testimonials could include:

> **Press releases** – issue a formal press release on a big customer win, either based on the size of the company win or the type of customer. Be sure to include a quote from the customer.

> **Video testimonial releases** – a video testimonial is a powerful tool that lets your customer share their story in their own words. Post it on YouTube, embed it on your website and share it on social media.

Podcasts – typically an audio recording that can be digitally shared, a podcast is a great way to capture a customer story when video is not possible.

Website and marketing materials – updated all appropriate sections of your website and marketing materials with new customer testimonial quotes.

Blog posts – expand on your customer testimonial by writing a full blog post about the customer story. This is a great way to elaborate on testimonial quotes to provide more details and background information. Be sure to use any photos or videos to add more interest to the post.

Social media – testimonials can be very easily and quickly shared across social media sites like Twitter, Facebook, LinkedIn and Google+. Social media sites are great for sharing the big news and the smaller stuff too – like brief testimonial comments received online or through review sites.

Again, your specific PR initiatives will depend on your business. For some companies, a customer testimonial could mean a significant win for your business and be worthy of a press release. Plan for how to make the most out of these opportunities so that you can use these customer wins to win you more.

For others, testimonials might be a good opportunity to pitch media about doing a story about your company. And then for other companies a testimonial may just be a good content producer for your company blog, social media and marketing materials… but still promotable.

Handling Negative Public Relations / Reviews

Since we are discussing creating testimonials for PR purposes, we should probably briefly review the flip side... when negative news, reviews or activity impacts your business.

Every company – large and small – should have a plan for handling any negative PR. For most small businesses it comes in the form of a bad review from a customer dissatisfied with your service or product. And in today's online world those bad reviews can travel fast.

First, actively monitor places where your customers are likely to review your business (you should be doing this for both good and bad reviews). Also set up a Google Alert to send you an email whenever your company name appears on a website.

Some tools to help you actively monitor your online brand for negative mentions include:

- Reputation.com
- SocialMention.com
- ViralHeat.com
- Topsy.com

Of course the best way to counter any negative reviews is by avoiding them in the first place. Have an active follow-up process to ensure customer satisfaction. A simple email follow-up asking about their satisfaction will usually suffice. If there are any issues address them immediately.

If the issue was a really big miss on your part, consider offering the customer special discounts or add-on services to try to make up for it.

Building a PR Pipeline within a Marketing Plan

The best way to ensure a PR pipeline is continually fed with new ideas and initiatives is by making it a part of your annual marketing plan. As you plan out marketing and promotional activities for the year, align a PR initiative or strategy with each item.

For example, if you have plans for a product promotional campaign after the roll-out of new products, then a product press release should be scheduled ahead of it. Also plan to have media outreach for new products.

Planning PR initiatives (such as press releases, media alerts or media briefings) around scheduled events or trade shows is another way to plan ahead. And don't forget about the post-event follow-up too.

Create an annual marketing plan and calendar that is seeded with important dates and activities for your business throughout the year. These could include things like seasonal peak periods, holiday sales, trade events, or planned product launches. Then, align basic public relations plans with each of these important dates and activities so that PR is always a part of your marketing effort.

Next Steps for Your PR Adventures

Like any part of marketing, PR is what you make of it. You may get lucky along the way with instant wins by being at the right place at the right time, but typically it takes some perseverance from you to make it happen.

As you go through the process of gathering testimonials, pitching story ideas to journalists and writing your own press releases managing your own PR will become routine. That first major pick-up from your key target publication will inspire you to get more. You will likely learn along the way that positive results typically produce more positive results. That positive momentum will continue to build and result in more inquiries, more publicity and more buzz for your small business.

Be sure to take advantage of the **bonus PR tools** available as free downloads. Direct links are located in the directory chapter of this book along with some other valuable public relations resources and tools.

Chapter 14: Directory of PR Marketing Tools and Resources

We have discussed a lot of different ideas and strategies throughout this book. Hopefully you feel confident enough to take on a more active role in PR activity and really begin to toot your own horn for your small business.

As you move forward with more public relations initiatives you may find that you need to take a deeper dive into one or more topics. To help you along the way, I've pulled together a listing of more tools and resources that you may find useful for reference.

Be sure to download the Bonus Free PR Tools developed specifically for use with this book. The bonus tools are templates that you can use to help you through the planning and implementation of press releases and media outreach. Sample data is also included with each template to show you how they are used.

FREE PR BONUS TOOLS
Download these PR tools developed by SBMarketingTools.com:

Press Release Checklist – a step-by-step checklist to help you throughout the press release creation, review and distribution process
- Download Checklist in Excel:
http://sbmarketingtools.com/i/u/10142294/f/PRToolsBook/Press_Release_Checklist.xlsx

- Download Checklist in PDF:
http://sbmarketingtools.com/i/u/10142294/f/PRToolsBook/Press_Release_Checklist.pdf

Press Release Template – a simple press release layout to structure important sections of company press releases
- Download Template in Word:
http://sbmarketingtools.com/i/u/10142294/f/PRToolsBook/Press_Release_template.docx

- Download Template in PDF:
http://sbmarketingtools.com/i/u/10142294/f/PRToolsBook/Press_Release_template.pdf

Media Outreach Guide – a guide to get organized with a media outreach plan by tracking contacts, outreach goals, strategies and ideas
- Download Guide in Excel:
http://sbmarketingtools.com/i/u/10142294/f/PRToolsBook/Media_Outreach_Guide.xlsx

- Download Guide in PDF:
http://sbmarketingtools.com/i/u/10142294/f/PRToolsBook/Media_Outreach_Guide.pdf

MORE PUBLIC RELATIONS RESOURCES

HARO (Help a Reporter Out) http://helpareporter.com
Get featured by news reporters by making yourself available as
an expert source for reporters looking for sources in news and
editorial stories.

Similar to HARO:
http://www.reporterconnection.com
http://www.flacklist.com
http://www.seekorshout.com
http://www.mymediainfo.com

PitchEngine - http://new.pitchengine.com/
PitchEngine offers a full suite of Web 2.0 tools for PR
professionals and journalists helping businesses create better
content to share via social networks, search engines and
mobile devices.

Public Relations Society of America (PRSA) –
http://www.prsa.org/
Learn more about the public relations industry, PR
terminology and best practices and identify PR agencies if
needed

Online Brand Management
Use these tools to monitor negative and positive mentions
about your company online:

- http://www.Reputation.com
- http://www.SocialMention.com
- http://www.ViralHeat.com
- http://www.Topsy.com

Blog / Content Building Tools

My Guest Blog http://www.MyGuestBlog.com - find guest blogging opportunities to promote your brand, or bloggers to submit content to your blog

Blog Dash http://www.blogdash.com – find and pitch blogs in your industry category for story coverage

Guestr – http://www.guestr.com – an exchange for website owners and writers to find guest post opportunities

Guest Blog Genius – http://www.guestbloggenius – find guest post opportunities to build your online authority

SEO Tools to Optimize PR Efforts:

Google Insights for Search –
http://www.google.com/insights/search/
Compare search engine volume for specific keywords by geographic area and categories to refine keyword selection.

Google AdWords: Keyword Tool –
https://adwords.google.com/o/Targeting/Explorer?_u=1000000000&_c=1000000000&ideaRequestType=KEYWORD_IDEAS#search.none
Get keyword phrase ideas based on competition and search volume

RECOMMENDED BOOKS

The AMA Handbook of Public Relations by Robert L. Dilenschneider and Maria Bartiromo (Feb 17, 2010)

The PR Buzz Factor: How Using Public Relations Can Boost Your Business by Russell Lawson (Feb 28, 2006)

The New Rules of Marketing & PR: How to Use Social Media, Online Video, Mobile Applications, Blogs, News Releases, and Viral Marketing to Reach Buyers Directly by David Meerman Scott

It's Not Who You Know -- It's Who Knows You!: The Small Business Guide to Raising Your Profits by Raising Your Profile by David Avrin

The Handbook of Strategic Public Relations and Integrated Communications by Clarke L. Caywood (May 1, 1997)

Planning and Managing Public Relations Campaigns: A Strategic Approach (PR in Practice) by Anne Gregory (Jul 28, 2010)

Public Relations Writing and Media Techniques (6th Edition) by Dennis L. Wilcox (Jan 3, 2009)

How to Write a Press Release (Second Edition) by Brian Cook

The Ultimate Press Release Swipe File – 50 Templates That You Can Use to Get Your Business Media Exposure Today by Steve Williams

SEO For 2012: Search Engine Optimization Secrets by Sean Odom and Lynell Allison

**For direct links to these books on Amazon, including a brief synopsis to review for each book, go to our PR books page here: http://sbmarketingtools.com/public-relations-books

Glossary of PR Terms

Advertising value equivalency (AVE): the amount in dollars a story would cost if it appeared as paid advertising in a publication and is typically determined by the size or length of the story by the advertising rate it would have cost for an equivalent ad size.

Audience: the target group of people you want to reach.

Backgrounder: a document containing background information on a person, organization, issue, etc. with more extensive information than generally available in publicity materials such as news releases.

Biography (Bio): a brief overview of a person's life typically focused on professional experience that lends expertise to a business.

Boilerplate: a brief paragraph stating who you are, what you do, and how you do it, usually used as the first paragraph in a biography or last paragraph in a news release

B-roll: a videotaped news story or video footage produced by an organization and distributed to television newsrooms. Also known as a Video News Release (VNR).

Buzz: refers to the excitement generated by media coverage or PR, often caused by a product, celebrity, company, etc. Good buzz can help keep a company in the news.

Byline: the name printed below the title of a newspaper or magazine article, crediting the author.

Circulation: the distribution of newspapers, magazines, and other print publications.

Clip or clipping: a story cut from a publication or a segment cut from a video or audiotape. Clips are good to showcase in the press room of your website.

Concept story: feature story designed to pique the interest of a certain demographic audience.

Copy editor: last editorial professional to see, review and approve written material before it is delivered to an audience by a media outlet.

Corporate fact sheet: one-page document that describes a company's executives, products and services, philosophy, markets served and company contact information.

Editorial: a statement of opinion from an editor or publisher about you and your business. Editorial is also used to refer to media coverage generated by news staff.

Editorial calendar: the listing of specific times (dates, months) a publication will focus on special sections, topics or special news reporting. Many trade and business trade publications plan content and themes up to a year in advance. An editorial calendar lists the special editorial focus for each issue.

Ghostwriter: person writing articles or speeches for another person who claims authorship.

Masthead: list of editors, publishers, and senior reporters in each publication's issue. A masthead is a good way to determine important editorial contacts.

Media: a general term that can refer to reporters, editors, and producers, or print publications, broadcast programs, and online magazines.

Media advisory: a written notice sent to media providing information (who, what, when, where, and why) on a news conference or other newsworthy event for potential coverage.

Media alert: a similar term for a media advisory - written notice sent to media providing information (who, what, when, where, and why), but generally for harder, more timely news.

Media contact list: a list of experts within your business, with the topics or subject matter on which they are qualified, made available to the media for interviews or story contributions.

Media kit: a package consisting of a news release and supporting documents that are usually bundled together in a two-pocket folder with the release on the right and supporting documents on the left.

Media directory or media listing: a thorough list of media contacts by geography, industry or specialty that includes key contact information and market/audience focus for publications or news outlets. This type of compiled listing information is typically available for purchase from media listing companies such as Marketwire.

Media outlet: a publication or broadcast program that transmits news and feature stories to the public through any distribution channel.

Media relevance: the criteria used to determine the relevance of a specific medium to the business' target audience – such as demographics or geography coverage.

Media tour: a client or an organization spokesperson is sent out to visit media outlets or brief key journalists for interviews and appearances.

News feature: a special story or article in a print publication or on a broadcast program that includes detail about concepts and ideas of specific market interest.

News conference: a media event organized to make an announcement directly to the news media. News conferences are typically tied to an event (such as trade show events or special company events).

Op-Ed: article written by an expert that is positioned on the page opposite the editorial page.

Pitch letter: a letter written to introduce a source and story idea to a member of the media in hopes of editorial or story coverage.

Photo opportunity: an opportunity for the media to obtain a photograph(s) or videotape footage of a newsworthy person/people and/or an interesting happening.

Press release: a formal announcement of company news and information that is released to publications, news outlets and websites for potential media coverage.

Press room: a centralized location (typically on a website for businesses) for organizing company information for media contacts, prospects and clients such as: company background, press releases, news coverage, media contacts, press-ready resources and more.

Public relations: a variety of strategies and tactics developed to create favorable opinion or media coverage for a person, event, or product that ultimately supports the company's bottom line.

Publication: newspaper, magazine, newsletter or website with information, news, and feature stories, usually produced to be sold or as a service to members of associations or organizations.

PR / Publicity stunt: an act that is obviously created to generate public relations and can be viewed negatively if the intent for publicity is considered disingenuous.

Reach: geographic area of the audience and the number of readers, listeners, or viewers who can access the media in any region.

Reprint: copy of an article that mentions you or your company. Reprints are ideal for company website press rooms and for use as sales and marketing material.

Specialized publication: industry-specific trade or professional publication focused on one core topic. These types of publications can be highly influential for your industry.

Spin: the point of view or bias you create in a story or news coverage.

Story treatment: how a story is treated in the media – such as a cover story, a running story (with coverage over multiple days), a one-shot mention, a story earning multiple mentions in one issue or one day on multiple media outlets.

Social media release (SMR): an enhanced news release that is augmented by interactive elements such as audio, video, social bookmarking links, photos, and RSS feeds.

Syndicated columnist: a journalist hired by publications or broadcast organizations to produce materials (written or spoken) about specific feature subjects.

Type of coverage: the context in which a story is presented in the media (news, opinion/commentary, community service, etc.). Other types of coverage can include editorial, news story, blog post, news brief, bumper, letter to the editor, comment to a blog post, etc.

Use of visuals: photos, images, charts and other illustrative information to supplement content in an article, story or news feature.

Video news release (VNR): a videotaped news story or video footage produced by an organization and distributed to television newsrooms or websites.

Wire or newswire service: news stories, features, etc., sent by direct line to subscribing or member news organizations (publications, newspapers, radio or television stations, news websites and more). Services such as Canadian Press (CP) or Associated Press (AP) are also called news wires and they feed their reports to newsroom websites.

About the Author

Diane Seltzer is a seasoned marketing communications, branding and social media consultant with a broad range of experience marketing a variety of industries and products.

With a diverse business background ranging from advertising account management to corporate marketing and marketing consulting, Diane offers a unique perspective on marketing strategies and implementation. Finding and effectively utilizing cost-effective marketing tools has been a focus throughout her career.

Diane is the founder of Small Business Marketing Tools – www.SBMarketingTools.com - a website devoted to marketing tools, resources and strategy ideas that offer free or low-cost small business solutions. Diane is also a freelance writer and marketing consultant for several small businesses.

PR Marketing Tools is the first in a series of books by *Small Business Marketing Tools* – a website focused exclusively on highlighting low-cost or free marketing tools, strategies and resources for small businesses.

You can keep updated on the latest small business marketing tools and resources – as well as new book titles – by subscribing to the monthly e-newsletter *Big Impact Ideas* at www.SBMarketingTools.com.

Connect with Me Online:

Twitter: http://twitter.com/SBMarketingTool

Google+ page:
https://plus.google.com/114835964625426883708

LinkedIn Group:
Small Business Marketing and Productivity Tools - http://www.linkedin.com/groups/Small-Business-Marketing-Productivity-Tools-4292201

Website: www.sbmarketingtools.com

DISCLAIMERS:

The strategies, ideas and advice expressed by the author of this book are intended for practical guidance for small business owners and entrepreneurs seeking to learn more about the topic. The author and SBMarketingTools.com makes no guarantees on the use of strategies or featured tools described in this book. Only companies that offer perceived valuable tools, services or products for small businesses are featured or recommended throughout this book or on SBMarketingTools.com.

www.ingramcontent.com/pod-product-compliance
Lightning Source LLC
Chambersburg PA
CBHW072036190526
45165CB00017B/956